HAPPINESS *Through* HARDSHIP

A Guide and Journal for Cancer
Patients, Their Caregivers and Friends
During an Initial Diagnosis

CARYN SULLIVAN

BALBOA.
PRESS

A DIVISION OF HAY HOUSE

Balboa Press books may be ordered through booksellers or by contacting:

Balboa Press
A Division of Hay House
1663 Liberty Drive
Bloomington, IN 47403
www.balboapress.com
1 (877) 407-4847

Because of the dynamic nature of the Internet, any web addresses or
links contained in this book may have changed since publication and
may no longer be valid. The views expressed in this work are solely those
of the author and do not necessarily reflect the views of the publisher,
and the publisher hereby disclaims any responsibility for them.

The author of this book does not dispense medical advice or prescribe the use
of any technique as a form of treatment for physical, emotional, or medical
problems without the advice of a physician, either directly or indirectly. The
intent of the author is only to offer information of a general nature to help
you in your quest for emotional and spiritual well-being. In the event you use
any of the information in this book for yourself, which is your constitutional
right, the author and the publisher assume no responsibility for your actions.

Any people depicted in stock imagery provided by Getty Images are
models, and such images are being used for illustrative purposes only.
Certain stock imagery © Getty Images.

Print information available on the last page.

ISBN: 978-1-9822-2756-2 (sc)
ISBN: 978-1-9822-2755-5 (hc)
ISBN: 978-1-9822-2757-9 (e)

Library of Congress Control Number: 2019906247

Balboa Press rev. date: 06/27/2019

Contents

Dedication

To my angels, Ellen, Mary Ann and Meghan, you showed me the light and how to live with and through cancer when I was first diagnosed. *This book is dedicated to you three.* You made this book possible because you guided me through those first few weeks and I lived through cancer gracefully and with joy.

To The Cancer Couch Foundation and Dr. Rebecca Timlin-Scalera, I'm in awe of your commitment to finding a cure or better treatments for stage IV disease. The Cancer Couch Foundation will help us and many more live and experience a better quality of life. Half of the profits of this book will be donated to The Cancer Couch Foundation.

Introduction

We have all experienced horribly gut-wrenching days, the kind that turn our worlds upside down and permanently alter our lives. For some, the initial reaction to being slapped across the face with such heartache is to collapse into a puddle of tears, while others go quiet, or fall into a state of shock, or even denial.

Any one of these reactions is expected and perfectly normal.

I was actually surprised at my initial reaction when diagnosed with cancer. I thought my world would crash after my first diagnosis at age 31 – and certainly after my second diagnosis with stage IV disease. But through the haze of anguish, fear, and the unknown, I realized I had a choice: *I could choose to be optimistic when hardship was thrown at me, or I could sink into a life of despair.* In the end, I chose optimism because I knew that **life could still provide joyful moments, even a little peace, while living with cancer.**

I'm here to share to all those touched by cancer that **above all else, there is hope.**

This book is meant to be a guide to help you, your caregiver, and your loved ones navigate the course of early diagnosis and find peace along the way. Whether you are the patient, the caregiver, a family member, or a friend, this book is to help you find happiness through the hardship. It can be done... It is a choice, and one that I truly believe is worth it.

I'm grateful that you selected this book and chose me to be your guide during this difficult time. I am also incredibly appreciative you bought this book because the proceeds of your purchase will support metastatic breast cancer research. I'm donating at least half of the net profits of *Happiness through Hardship* to The Cancer Couch Foundation, a non-profit organization that funds state-of-the art research labs solely focused on finding better treatments for metastatic breast cancer. As a cancer thriver living with stage IV disease, I always want to see the hope, love, and possibilities. This lifestyle, coupled with the results of research will help me and thousands of others live longer, better quality lives. It's what results out of the research that is the key that's paving the way for better treatments. This will be the ticket to live longer with late-stage cancer.

The Calm Before the Storm

I was lying in bed. The sun shined radiantly through my bedroom window. It was late 2004, just a few weeks before the winter holidays. While it was frigid outside, I was warm inside, clad in a tank top and pajama shorts and snuggled up close to my husband.

I was so comfortable. I was so happy. And I had so much to be happy about: *Two months earlier, I had married my Prince Charming.* Now we were about to celebrate the holidays in our new home, and I was perfectly content enjoying everything about being Kevin's wife.

I turned over and kissed my new husband on the cheek, secretly hoping this would awaken him. It didn't, so I laid there for a while thinking how lucky I was to be married to my best friend. Once Kevin woke up, our pillow talk wasn't comprised of the usual laughing at stories of our friends' antics, dreaming up our future family, or detailing our next career endeavors. On this

1

morning, we giggled about pain after I complained to him about an ache in my side.

I was still on a fitness "high," reeling off of months of prepping for our wedding. My strenuous workouts involved a weekly kickboxing, running, and weightlifting regimen, so I assumed the pain was from this overexertion. Finally – on the morning of December 20, to be exact – I mentioned to my husband that I planned to see a doctor for my pain. He recommended if I was going to see a doctor, that I first have to get a lump on my breast checked out. He nonchalantly said, "You should get one of those mammogram things." I gaffed at him – "Ugh, Kevin, those are for old people." However, I listened, and made a doctor's appointment the next day to discuss the lump.

I never worried about going to the doctor because in my mind, I would visit physicians just so they could tell me I was healthy. I wanted to do due-diligence and check it out, but I truly believed I would be fine.

Chapter 2

The First Few Days

I went to see my primary care doctor on December 21, and because I didn't think it would turn out to be anything, I went by myself.

The doctor looked at the lump and recommended standard tests and protocol. *No problem.* So, on that day, I had a mammogram and an ultrasound. After, the doctor told me there wasn't anything alarming on the mammogram or ultrasound. However, because I was young, and my breast tissue was dense, he ordered a fine needle biopsy.

I had the biopsy procedure done within a few days. I still was thinking, *standard protocol. No big deal.*

Luckily, the doctor and nurse didn't put too many scary ideas in my head about the "what ifs." I had friends' moms who had been diagnosed with cancer, but many were in their sixties at the time of diagnosis. It didn't seem possible that breast cancer could be an option since I was in my early thirties, so my husband and I really didn't talk much about this being a "true" cancer scare.

We were very caught up in the last-minute chaos of the holiday season, not the possibilities of what this lump could be.

On December 28, I came home from work and went about my pre-dinner routine like I did most days. I was still waiting for my results, but I wasn't worried; I assumed the test results took a while.

Before dinner, I took a shower. When I got out, I discovered a voicemail message on my cell phone had popped up from my doctor. It was cryptic, and my heart sank. The doctor had a slight sense of urgency in his voice when he told me to call him tomorrow morning.

My mind wandered...

If it was good news, wouldn't he have said it in the message?

And...

If it was bad news, would he have wanted to wait until tomorrow to talk to me?

Question after question raced through my mind. My husband arrived home from work and I shared the news. While my stomach tightened with anxiety, my husband didn't worry. He seldom got worked up over any woe until it became certain. He suggested we watch a movie to pass the time instead of letting the worry get the best of me. I embraced the opportunity to be consumed by the silly comedy of Will Ferrell in "Elf."

The next morning, I headed to work early as usual. During the commute, I received a call requesting I come in before work. My heart raced, and my mind volleyed between calm and craziness. Once again, in a split second, many questions swirled my mind: *Why did the doctor need to see me* now? *Why couldn't this wait until lunchtime?*

My mind continued to wander as I turned the car around and drove to the doctor's office. While I was worried, I still didn't think it would be cancer. I was young (31,) fit, and healthy, with no family history of breast cancer.

I checked in and sat quietly by myself until a nurse escorted me into the back. As I sat in the stiff waiting room chair, my heart beat a little faster and my mind still raced with questions: *What could be wrong? Maybe I will need surgery to get rid of this lump?* When I heard the doctor talking right outside my door, the sound of his jolly tone convinced me the news he was about to deliver wouldn't be life-threatening. *Oh, the mind games we play,* I chastised myself. (Nonetheless, I still had anxiety in the pit of my stomach.)

Once the doctor finally entered the room, he sat down on the chair next to me, put his warm hand on my arm and explained, in what seemed to be slow motion, that he had never "done this" before. I knew he was a relatively new doctor, but this information was confusing, and so I thought, *Done what?*

Then, with his eyes glued to the sheet of paper in his other hand, he read me to me, "Invasive ductal carcinoma"…blah, blah…blah.

Those first three words, clad as they were in medical jargon, didn't mean anything to me. However, the somber tone in my doctor's voice and nervousness in his body language communicated to me clearly that "carcinoma" was bad.

The energy around me instantly changed. On the outside, my body looked calm as I stared motionlessly at the doctor as he re-read the diagnosis to me three times. But inside, I felt my gut flip and spin. The heaviness of this information took over, and my body felt instantly stripped of emotion. A dim haze surrounded me, smothering me, and I had no idea what I should do next. The doctor suggested I call my husband; he then left the room to give me some privacy.

My mind said, *Okay, so I have a bad diagnosis, but I'm here by myself. What do I do? Seriously…what do I do now??*

And…*I didn't know.* So, I just sat in the room by myself, looking out the window into the gray parking lot. Finally, somehow, I managed to call my husband from the room. I muttered that the news was bad; that I had cancer and that he should come to the doctor's office now.

Kevin hung up and immediately left home to meet me.

During the hour it took him to get to the doctor's office, I was still sitting alone in the private room, my thoughts were unclear. I grappled with whether I should reschedule my workday. I didn't really know what to do, so I just stood in the doctor's office looking out the window. *Alone.* No one came in to check on me during that time...not the doctor, not the nurses. I didn't leave to take a bathroom break or walk around the office. I just stood there. Waiting. In limbo.

As I looked out the window confused yet calm, my reflexes urged me to call someone who could help me. I wanted Kevin there. I wanted some clarity on what this cancer diagnosis meant. While I didn't know what to do...I wanted to do something. So, I ended up calling my college best friend, Meghan, whose mother was a breast cancer survivor. It's ok to be still and do nothing and it's also ok to do something. In reflection, I was being true to myself – connecting with people who brought me good energy and providing me with valuable information to make my situation better.

Once my husband arrived and the nurse brought him in to join me, the doctor returned, sat down on his chair next to us, and shared the diagnosis again. This time, he gave us a packet with detailed information, including next steps on how to meet oncologists and surgeons who could help us move forward on this cancer journey.

After we left the doctor's office, the news still didn't settle in. We had heard the diagnosis, but couldn't comprehend the overturning of our lives that was about to happen. We didn't know where to go and were unsure of what to do in those initial moments. I mean, *Who* could *think clearly? What do you* do *when first diagnosed with cancer?*

And then...my stomach growled. Kevin and I looked at

each other, almost questioning whether we should eat. With the heaviness of the situation surrounding us, I wasn't sure we were going to be comfortable being in public.

First, we drove to Kevin's work to drop off his car, so we could be together for the drive home. We then chose to grab bagel sandwiches and eat in the car, even though we didn't talk.

As I finished my lunch, I realized we had parked near my favorite makeup store. In that moment, my heart fluttered, and I laughed. *It seemed ridiculous to want to go shopping for a new lipstick...or was it?* I decided it's what I wanted to do, so I walked in the store smiling. Not because I was happy, but because I was happy to be somewhere that took my thoughts away from cancer. I spoke to the saleswoman, and she shared her favorite colored glosses for the season, ones that would really sparkle for New Year's. I tried on a few different lipstick shades and decided on one.

As she and I conversed, I was really only present for half the dialogue. My mind felt as if it was standing outside my body and watching the interaction. My thoughts ran like this...*Isn't it funny that this lady thinks I'm young and fun, and my only care is about a lipstick for New Year's? Little does she know I was just diagnosed with cancer a few hours earlier.*

Once the sale of the lipstick was completed, I thanked her, left the store with my new shade, and sank back into the passenger seat next to Kevin.

As we drove home again, that same kind of conversation went on in my head over the next few hours. We stopped at a stoplight, and I looked at another car's driver: *I bet he doesn't even know that I have cancer.* As we pulled up into our driveway, the neighbors down the road waved, figuring we were just home from work early. *They don't know the doctor told me I have cancer.*

No one could see my insides. They didn't know my world had been turned upside down.

This kind of mental dialogue would happen a lot over the first few weeks.

Then Kevin and I were home. Out of the haze of that first day, the reality and fear had finally sunk in. The rest of the world was moving forward – and I had cancer.

The first twenty-four hours were the worst. In the dark aka scary hours, the bizarre haze morphed into fear. A whole lot of overwhelming fear…

Fear of dying.

Fear of the unknown.

Fear of dying.

Fear of hair loss.

Fear of dying.

Fear of crazy medicine and weird side effects.

Fear of dying.

Fear of infertility.

Fear of dying.

Fear of depression.

Fear of dying.

That night, shaking with overflowing tears, Kevin held me tightly in his arms. He eventually fell asleep, but I couldn't.

I tossed back and forth in bed the whole night. My body felt heavy, and my thoughts were scattered: *I can't believe I have cancer. Who gets cancer this young? Am I going to die? Will I ever get to see my thirty-second birthday?* These thoughts rummaged and pillaged through my head. Then, my superhero self would try and squash those thoughts: *Okay, I have cancer. I don't know anything yet, but I will. I may not die. And I don't want to die.*

I didn't realize then that this moment was one of clarity: **All I cared about, at my core, was living.**

As the random thoughts continued to race through my head, I finally saw a light. I thought about a woman I knew locally, older than me, but still young to have breast cancer. She was a soap opera actress, a mother, a school advisor, and a beam of light. She smiled a lot, laughed big and taught at my nephew's school.

Once I had watched her lead a whole kindergarten graduation ceremony. With a bright pink scarf wrapped around a bald head and a radiant sparkle in her eyes, she greeted every student with a mini-diploma and a huge hug. She raced around the room making sure the slide show projector was working, the snacks were displayed, and the guests had enough seats. She did all of this while in the midst of chemotherapy and only months out of surgery. She was truly vibrant, and it was clear she loved life.

I started thinking, *If Mary Ann could do it, I can too. If Mary Ann could do it, I can too.* I said this to myself for at least an hour. I was able to push all the bad thoughts away while I whispered this chant.

Curled up in bed, chanting in my head during those first few late-night hours on my diagnosis day, I realized all I cared about was *not dying.*

I decided to focus thereafter **on learning everything I could to make sure I was going to stay alive.**

When it comes to the initial diagnosis, you can't bury your head in the sand for long. It's unfortunate, but you have to make several decisions in a short amount of time.

Truth be told, there were many roller coasters I encountered along the way. The first few weeks after my diagnosis were the most stressful, and extremely draining mentally. I was blessed that other survivors – I call them, "my angels" – helped provide me with guidance so that I could make smart decisions for myself.

Ultimately, you have to make the decisions for yourself with the information you have at the time. I believe in being prepared and thorough, so you can be happy with the decisions you make.

Helpful Hints

Patient Tips:

Just be, just breathe – Do whatever you need to do (within legal reason) to get through the day.

Journal if you are able – It's cathartic, and you never know if you will want or need the words describing this experience at some other point in time. See the back of this book for journal pages.

Caregiver Tips:

Listen, just listen, to the patient.

Start to gather the next steps in the treatment search.

Chapter 3

Your Coping and Care

On Day Two with cancer, I woke up wondering if I was ready to begin my new life as "Caryn with Cancer" – and simply not knowing what to do with such earth-shattering news.

Those first twenty-four hours were the worst – and the next day was pretty rotten as well. But I was determined to turn things around, so I thought about how I handled hard times earlier in my life.

While a cancer diagnosis differs from a broken finger, stressful boss, or some kind of social/relationship drama, there is an effective tool I've used in situations and conflicts throughout my life. I call it my "mourning-without-care" period, and I give myself a certain amount of time – usually forty-eight hours – to mourn without care.

If that meant staying in bed and crying all day and night, then that's what I would do.

If it meant feeling sorry for myself and talking about it for two straight days, then I did it.

If it was locking myself in a room and blasting music…eating too much…eating too little…swearing, dancing, or just *being* – as long as it wasn't against the law or incredibly unhealthy – I was okay with it and I did it.

Then, after my mourning-without-care time period, I take one step at a time and bring my life back in focus. I create a to-do list and then start working things off the list in priority order.

And trust me, that's *exactly* what I did when the shock of my cancer diagnosis struck. The headaches, tissue-scratched nose, and mind-racing negativity momentarily pained me, but I didn't judge myself for them. *I just let them be until I moved on – and then I felt relieved to be freed from them.*

You see, with a cancer diagnosis, there isn't a lot of time to just "sit back." You have to figure out the treatment plan – which can be daunting. In the long run, the research and information-gathering will likely make the situation less stressful and ease your mind somewhat. *Less stress = peace = happiness.* To this day, I am confident with my treatment plan because it was well thought out. I'm happy with the decisions my husband and I made, and grateful for the family, friends, and doctors who helped make it happen.

Part of coping successfully with the hardship of disease involves finding a care team. A *care team* consists of people you want to be your support system. Specifically, it is the people you know who will provide help, guidance, and authentic support. (It's not just a list of people who say they "want" to be there for you. It's those who *will*.)

It's important to put together a solid team because you will need to draw on their help during treatment to make your life easier. In doing so, consider these questions:

"Who makes your life easier?"
- You can find a role for them, even if they live far away.

"Who is exceptionally organized?"
- They can potentially take notes, attend your appointments with you, or even arrange for other friends to help you with your family or work situation.

"Who makes you laugh?"
- FaceTime them every other day.

"Can they come visit once a week?"
- When they do, you can talk about anything *other than cancer*. Let them try to bring you back to "normalcy."

"Who has been through this before?"
- They can be your new pen pal/text pal, providing insight when you need it.

While it's no fun to be going through turmoil, *being surrounded by loved ones and people who selflessly care will make the experience less stressful*. It's easy to feel love when people care.

When I feel loved, I am truly happy.

So, what I found out early in my cancer adventure is this: **Cancer is devastating, but it doesn't mean I (or you) have to be devastated.**

Helpful Hints

Patient Tips:

Who brings positive energy in your life? – Don't overthink this. Who always sends you love and makes you smile? Once you have your answer, let them know about your situation. This will help you feel love and secure throughout difficult times. Keep these people close, creating an inner circle of support.

Caregiver Tips:

Always be aware of your audience. Be yourself, but also be mindful of what you say – Don't say things that might not be true, like, "It's going to be okay," or, "I know you are going to get through this." Instead, *just listen*. Offer to them that you are there. For example, "This must be hard for you. I'm here if you want to talk about it." And, "I will be here to support you during treatment."

Think how you can help *proactively* – When you ask someone as to what they need, often they will reply, "Nothing." (They may decline your offer now because they think they will *really* need your help later, and so do not want to bother you at this early moment.) Well, being proactive can lessen their load *right now*.

What does it mean to *proactively help*? Instead of asking the patient "what they need" or "what you can do for them," individually and uniquely offer a specific gesture, or drop off a gift at their home, without even asking! If you are the chief caregiver, spreading the "be proactive" message to all the patient's family and friends is key, so those who care know not to wait to hear from the patient.

50 thoughtful
GIFT IDEAS & GESTURES

Pretty WELLNESS

1. A handwritten personal note
2. An upbeat playlist
3. Art made by your kids
4. A goofy poem
5. A video card made in iMovie
6. A collage of old and new photos
7. A collage from magazines of inside jokes or funny childhood heart throbs
8. A weekly themed text: Throwback Thursday with old pictures or Motivation Monday for inspirational notes
9. A basket of entertainment magazines
10. Cozy new pajamas
11. Comfortable new yoga or sweat pants
12. A basket full of organic teas or coffee
13. A fruit basket from Edible Arrangements
14. An herb, tomato or small vegetable potted plant
15. An organic fruit subscription
16. Your favorite funny book – hardcover or audio version
17. Silly and colorful high socks or reflexology socks
18. Soups – fresh (or frozen can be shipped)
19. An iTunes gift card with a note listing your favorite happy songs, books or apps
20. An iTunes, Best Buy or Amazon gift card with a list of your favorite funny movies
21. A grocery store gift card – one with online delivery
22. A gift certificate to a local restaurant that delivers
23. Toys, books or any present for her child
24. A family board game
25. Decks of cards – even get them personalized with family photos
26. A yearly magazine subscription
27. A yearly app subscription like Headspace for a peaceful meditation practice
28. A Netflix subscription
29. An Amazon Prime subscription (or gift card for an additional year)

50 thoughtful
GIFT IDEAS & GESTURES

Pretty WELLNESS

30. Sentimental items to serve as her good luck charms – healing crystals or trinkets
31. A beautiful box to store sentimental items during this journey
32. A fancy notebook or journal
33. Eye masks and pads for better sleep and pain relief
34. Send a note with a list of days you are free to come over and babysit her kids
35. Send a note with a list of days you are free to come over and tidy her house
36. Send a note with a list of days you are free to run errands or drive carpools
37. Organize a dinner caravan like MealTrain.com
38. Offer to make her kids lunches for a week
39. Offer to take her to a makeup boutique and get a cancer makeover with makeup that will make her feel better through treatment
40. Offer to attend appointments or meetings
41. Offer to research topics for her: foods to eat during treatment, medication side effects or other questions she may want answered
42. Offer to create a list of companies that support her hospital or diagnosis
43. Hire and pay for a cleaning service for her
44. Buy or make a scarf
45. Buy or make a cozy blanket
46. Hire a personal trainer to go to her house
47. Hire a yoga instructor to go to her house
48. Come up with a list of YouTube videos for exercise or yoga
49. Send a care package for her to bring to her treatments to "treat the doctors/nurses" who care for her
50. Donate to a charity in her honor

Chapter 4

"Google is Not My Doctor"

As I was leaving the doctor's office on the day I was diagnosed, the staff recommended I not go to the internet for information.

Huh… My gut instinct had been to jump on the computer and Google everything I could about cancer once I got home.

You see, at that time I was filled with uncertainty and holding a pile of 'official' handouts; I, well, I didn't know how to wrestle through the information. I thought it might be easier to Internet-surf for more accessible language and anecdotal stories.

But their advice was good, and I'm glad I listened.

I say the same to you: **DON'T DO IT.**

Oftentimes, computer algorithms will provide websites, blogs, and information that have the highest traffic, not necessarily the right or most pertinent information. It's much better to *enlist your support team to do some research, especially when it comes to searching the Internet.*

My sister was my research support team. She lived far away and loved investigating information for me because it meant she could make a difference, despite living thousands of miles away. So, she scoured medical journals to get data on breast cancer drug trials, while also researching the results on new protocols for cancer patients. In doing all this, she put my mind at ease, and I had all the information handy for when I needed it. Her contributions were invaluable and allowed me to concentrate on the immediate decisions and my day-to-day needs.

While it seems like a no-brainer, another piece of advice I received early on was to find the best medical team, so I would have faith in the decisions we made together. The key word here is "WE." While having the right medical team is essential, always know this is *your* life and *you* make the decisions. You have to be an advocate for yourself because only *you* know what you are feeling. Only *you* know deep down how you really want to live your life.

So, how did I find my medical team?

I sought out second, third and even fourth opinions. I saw doctors at the hospital that diagnosed me, but I also asked around to local friends who were touched by cancer to see if they had any suggestions. And they did…

I was diagnosed on December 29, 2004. The day after the diagnosis, Kevin and I were driving to an appointment when my phone rang. It was my friend, Trish. I answered the phone, figuring it might be a nice diversion.

Trish asked what we had been up to lately and questioned why we didn't attend our friend's holiday party the week prior. Due to the giggle in her voice and light tone, I knew she was hinting at whether Kevin and I might be announcing a pregnancy soon. Wanting to stop those thoughts before they grew further, I told her the truth: "We missed the party because of a surgical biopsy, and I was just diagnosed with breast cancer." Without a beat she said, "Caryn, my mom has nine friends who have had breast cancer, and they are all still living. I'm getting off the phone right now to call her, and she will call you back. Are you okay with that?"

Twenty minutes later, when Trish's mom, Ellen, called, she had already made me an appointment with a breast surgeon for a second opinion. Kindly, Ellen shared that she wanted to help me move forward, and that I could cancel the meeting at any time.

Trish's proactivity and Ellen's ability to connect me up with my immediate needs were invaluable gifts. The new doctor's appointment gave me an opportunity to share my diagnosis and potential treatment plan with another specialist.

At each new and subsequent appointment, I interviewed the doctors as if I was hiring a prospective employee to work for me. *Oh, wait - I WAS literally hiring this medical team to work ON me and for me.*

What happens when you don't have a Trish or an Ellen to advise you on who to approach for a second opinion?

It doesn't have to be difficult to find new opinions. Think of it simply as...*a networking project.*

Yes, of course it's another step to take, and it can be overwhelming, *but this is where your support team comes in.* Have them think about who they know that might be familiar with a good doctor/specialist in the area. Or, call a friend or close family to see if they are willing to reach out to anyone connected to a smart doctor related to your disease. If you have a child, call their pediatrician and ask for recommendations; they are likely to be aware of well-regarded specialists for both adults and children. Think about if you're willing and ready to speak with local cancer survivors to find out the names of their medical team members; if you don't know who they are, ask others in the neighborhood if they know of anyone.

Keep in mind this step provides an opportunity to ask others to help. Ask them to do some legwork; ask them to research other doctors. **Don't be shy.** This is why you have created this support team around you.

Coming up with a good medical team that I trusted didn't always mean I loved all the doctors – or even that I had to keep them. As cancer goes, your treatments may change, and if they do, then you need to reassess whether your doctor(s) is the right one for you. I always wanted to find *the* medical expert, someone not just in the field of breast cancer, but also someone who specialized in whatever treatment I was receiving.

Additionally, I considered **my medical team to be *any* professional who was focusing on my health.** So, my team included my medical oncologist, breast surgeon, plastic surgeon, and radiation oncologist, as well as a naturopath, dietician, and yogi.

As expected, life after a cancer diagnosis can be overwhelming and exhausting, with appointments and a rollercoaster of emotions. At times, it feels like coordinating second and third consultations is simply…impossible. To combat this, I strongly suggest designating a few people to be in charge of organizing your cancer life. Friends and family members want to help, so consider asking a few reliable and bright people to coordinate research and tasks that you need.

Helpful Hints

Patient Tips:

Get hard copies of results – Ask your doctor to provide you with copies of your results (all notes and any images from any scans). If the doctor cannot provide them, call the Medical Records department at the hospital to receive the documents. You will need these documents for future appointments, and it's important to have your own record. Some hospitals provide Electronic Health Record (EHR) systems. Sign up for such a service, so you have instant access to most of your files.

Create a health binder or folder – You will be getting a lot of information at all of your doctors' appointments, and you will want to keep all of the records together.

Ask the doctor you are seeing at the time for recommendations for other doctors and specialists, depending on your hardship – Mine included: breast surgeon, oncologist, radiation oncologist, dietician/nutritionist, and physical therapist, among others. Don't leave the office without scheduling another appointment with them. Get a list of potential doctors and specialists to see.

Delegate to close friends – They want to help, so *let them*. Come up with a list of tasks you want done, and *delegate*. If you're overwhelmed, designate a 'chief caregiver' to take the lead and have them communicate on your behalf. One of the areas of greatest help to me was when **friends researched the modalities the doctors were talking about, including surgery options,**

side effects, treatments, and success stories. Ask friends to send you information that is digestible. Let *them* go to the Internet, NOT YOU. There is a tremendous amount of scary (i.e., not even correct) information out there, so let them weed through it.

Consider finding an "appointment buddy" — During the first few weeks after diagnosis, shock, stress, and exhaustion really take over. It's beneficial to have a person attending your appointments with you to take notes and/or help provide support when you need to make decisions. Choose this person wisely or consider having a few different attendees. Having a great note-taker with you is important in the beginning when you are considering different treatments. As my surgeries and appointments ramped up, I found having someone who was nurturing alongside me worked well.

Caregiver Tips:

Get hard copies of results – Ask the patient if you can help gather their results.

Research/ask around for recommended doctors, specialists, and natural practitioners who could help the patient – Provide the patient with one list in a Word/Google document/email.

Offer to gather information – Research treatments/side effect and success stories.

Create a comprehensive family health history document – Include information dating back to grandparents and their respective health information, if available.

Gather success stories – Oftentimes, even if the initial diagnosis is a "common" one, the patient feels like they are the *only one* experiencing it, when in reality, they're not. Finding others who've had success with the same disease is a good step for a caregiver. Having said that, don't send to the patient until it makes sense to share; flooding them with other people's stories may be overwhelming.

Gather and share inspirational quotes – Find out if your friend prefers texts, emails, or snail mail, then send motivational quotes this way to them to keep them going. Check out BrainyQuotes. com for ideas.

Gather titles of inspirational books – If you know your friend well, buy them one of the inspirational books you've found. If you don't know them well enough, an Amazon gift card with book recommendations is thoughtful. Easy and quick reads worked best for me; they were easy to digest in a time period of confusing and detailed information. Some of the books that got me through included Kris Carr's *Crazy Sexy Cancer* and David Servan-Schreiber's *Anticancer.*

Chapter 5

How to Call the Shots

My first cancer diagnosis truly was my adulthood awakening. Every decision I made before then was fairly easy and likely in my control. Cancer wasn't, though. But I still had to deal!

I wish I had all the answers – or better yet, a crystal ball. I can't tell you what to do and/or how to do it. What was right for me may not be right for you. However, I believe that *preparation* will provide insight and direction on how to make the hard decisions.

Because of organization and preparation, I was less stressed and able to experience a little joy throughout my cancer journey.

I'm proud of the decision-making process I've used to date. It's pretty universal and consistent in terms of how I've evaluated opportunities throughout my entire life, including as a prospective college student, young employee rising the corporate ladder, and breast cancer patient vetting life-saving actions. And through it all – and while the topic at hand can be overwhelming… I always try to keep it simple:

1. I list all my options (treatment options, doctors, medications, etc.).
2. I thoroughly research the pros/cons of each option - often allowing others to help me gather the information, both anecdotal and data-driven.
3. I start vetting which treatments (or situations) seem to fit my needs.
4. I talk, talk, and talk again to people in similar situations. Not just cancer survivors, but those who have information that can help bring useful ideas.

Eventually, I (and you) will have a direction, which should make my (and your) choosing easier.

As for me, after going through this decision-making process, I ultimately decided for a bilateral mastectomy, reconstructive surgery, and Adriamycin/Cytoxan/Taxol chemotherapy. Given the research and vast amount of information with which Kevin and I were armed, I was satisfied and confident that my husband and I were making all the right decisions.

While the first several weeks were draining both emotionally and physically, I also was incredibly relieved once treatment started. Being a newlywed wrestling through all these big life decisions was daunting, but I did it, together with my husband.

We took each decision and mapped it out.

We spoke to survivors, doctors, and family to receive feedback.

However, at some point, we needed to call the shots – and we did.

Helpful Hints

Note pages are in the back of this book that can be used at your appointments. Bookmark this page with questions and take notes here or in the back of the book so they are all in one place, easy for you to use.

List of Questions to Ask Doctors When Evaluating Treatments

Can you please explain my illness?

What type is it?

Where is it located? *(if this applies)*

What are the risk factors for this illness?

Are my family members at risk? If so, what should they do?

Tell me about your hopeful patients and success stories.

What diagnostic tools have you used/should you use for my case?

Are there any side effects from using these?

How often will you monitor me long-term with these tools?

Where do I go?

How should I prepare for them?

What is your recommendation for treatment?

Why?

What are the pros/cons of this treatment?

What are the side effects?

What are my options for managing the side effects?

Will my other activities and lifestyle activities (e.g., diet, exercise, etc.) need to be changed as a result of starting with this treatment?

How have your patients fared on this treatment (side-effects-wise)?

How will this influence my life over the short term and long term?

What is the expected timeline until I start the treatment? Through the entire treatment?

What are my other options for treatment?

How many patients like me have you treated?

How much experience do you and your team have with patients with my particular case?

Do you have a cancer care team or other doctors/nurses/people who will support me during my illness?

Can you explain their roles?

Are there other support services available to me and my family?

Does the hospital offer counseling, nutrition guidance, massage, reiki, or integrative medicine?

Do you take calls after hours or send emails to your patients?

Do you encourage your patients to call or email with questions?

Is there a person who can talk me through managing the costs of this illness?

Whom in your office handles health insurance concerns?

Chapter 6

What About the Money?

For some, money is a subject that is incredibly hard to discuss openly. Yet when hardship hits – especially one that is life-threatening – questions about money often come up: *Will I have enough? Will this put me into debt? How much will these treatments cost? Will my insurance cover my appointments, treatments, preventative scans, and medications?* The list goes on and on...

Well, because everyone's cancer or illness is different, their individual treatment plan is different, and likely their insurance too. So while I don't have any guarantees, I do know about options.

First and foremost, **talk to your insurance provider.** *If you don't have insurance, or your insurance company doesn't cover everything, call the hospital and speak to someone in billing.* There are immediate options that can be discussed, ranging from hospital payment plans to overall reduced fees.

Once you understand your options, *call upon a service like CancerCare.* They offer financial assistance for cancer-related costs – including transportation and childcare. They also offer oncology social workers who can help you navigate the resources available for cancer patients.

There are local charities and centers that offer programs and grants for patients as well.

When it comes to purchasing medications, know that *some of the big pharmaceutical companies offer coupons online*. It's also worth a call to better understand any patient programs offered by the Big Pharma companies. Sometimes the reductions and programs aren't promoted, but the opportunities exist.

Last but certainly not least, *caregivers and friends can create opportunities to lighten the financial burden*. Clearly, monetary gift cards can help in many ways and creating fundraisers can garner immediate cash. In recent years, GoFundMe pages have become incredibly popular, and are a viable option for raising funds.

I know that suggesting such comes with emotional ties: It's hard to admit to those close to you that money is tight. And, no matter how much or how little money you have, accepting money and gifts can make you vulnerable. But trust me, friends and family members want to help – and often don't know how. Because there's an unknown with cancer financing, having a friend create a GoFundMe page is an option to raise money virtually without you having to ask someone directly for a loan. And with all the stress and red tape of health insurance, it can give a patient a bit more peace of mind to have some additional funds in their pockets to pay for their treatments.

Resources for Treatment & Financial Decisions:

PrettyWellness.com – I created this website to share my inspiring stories, and treatment and health tips, for cancer patients and survivors - **http://prettywellness.com/cancer-resources/**

Art therapy – Contact a local hospital to inquire about programs or check out this one – **https://www.mskcc.org/experience/patient-support/activities/art-therapy**

CancerCare – Information on available support groups, financial assistance, and counseling - **http://CancerCare.org**

Cancer Connect – Online community for patients and caregivers - **CancerConnect.com**

Chemotherapy Thoughts – Chemotherapy info - **http://pretty wellness.com/chemotherapytips/**

Chemotherapy – Saving Hair – **https://www.breastcancer.org/tips/hair_skin_nails/cold-caps**

Cleaning for a Reason – Free home cleaning for patients - **http://cleaningforareason.org**

Clinical trials – Finding them – **https://www.cancer.gov/about-cancer/treatment/clinical-trials**

Free products/services for patients – https://www.cancerhorizons.com/free-stuff/

Healing Meals / Ceres Community Project – Meals that nourish critically ill patients and empower teens - http://healingmealsproject.org and https://www.ceresproject.org

Home matters and cancer – A guide to keeping your home through illness - https://www.mortgagecalculator.org/helpful-advice/keeping-your-home.php

Look Good, Feel Better Program – complimentary beauty – http://LookGoodFeelBetter.org

Money – GoFundMe campaigns – https://www.gofundme.com

Oncology Medical Community – https://www.onclive.com

Overall caregivers, family, and friends support – https://www.cancer.gov/about-cancer/coping/caregiver-support?redirect=true

Radiation therapy – https://www.cancer.gov/about-cancer/treatment/types/radiation-therapy

Research and Angel Funds – http://TheCancerCouch.com

Wigs – How to choose a wig – https://www.dana-farber.org/health-library/articles/how-to-choose-a-wig/

Young Survival Coalition – Understanding treatments, scans, and reports - https://www.youngsurvival.org/learn/living-with-breast-cancer/understanding-treatment

Chapter 7

In the Thick of Treatment

The first few weeks, Kevin and I just focused on practical matters like figuring out treatments and creating a plan. And although those practical matters were much more stressful than I could have ever imagined, it passed.

We created a plan.

We figured out the schedule.

We researched what preparations were necessary.

We were organized, and it helped lessen the stress of the situations ahead of us.

We packed our bags for day-visits or overnight hospital stays with comfortable PJs, music playlists and mindless magazines.

We worked through all the cancer activities – and then they became routine.

You, too, will come up with a plan. Likely, the first few weeks of doctor's appointments may have proved tiring and emotionally draining. (No one plans for cancer, and the researching doctors and treatment period takes priority over everything else in life.) Once you've decided on your treatments, though, the clouds part and a little sun shines through the darkness.

The idea of surgery, a bilateral mastectomy with reconstruction, terrified me. I couldn't envision a doctor putting me to sleep medically and cutting apart my body. Up to this point in my life, I had barely broken a bone and my aches had been minor, so I had never really felt deep physical pain.

Chemotherapy scared me the most. I envisioned myself hugging the porcelain toilet, afraid of throwing up all over the floor. I saw myself curling up on the bathroom floor and falling asleep, too tired to crawl into bed after chemo treatments.

Guess what? That scenario never happened. My imagination conjured up scary nightmares that never came true. The first few weeks after diagnosis and then the first treatments, there was truly a teeter-totter between fear and fine. And mostly, it was fine.

As cliché as it sounds, what I learned was *to take one day at a time.*

Some days I had to be a patient. Rest. Take the pills when I felt pain. Just sit still and let my body heal.

Other days, I felt okay. I could laugh at a silly sitcom or enjoy friends coming over to visit. This helped me mentally.

The "firsts" are often scary – but I came to learn that chemo, surgery, and radiation all were much easier than my wildest fears! If I had a bad day or two, I went through it, but didn't overwhelm myself with the notion that life was BAD. Having cancer was devastating, but I would not let it devastate me.

What else did I learn during treatment?

I learned that being a hero wasn't important. If I felt pain, I took meds. When concerned about anything, I called the doctors. (A lot.)

I learned to trust others, especially my medical team.

I learned to ask a lot of questions so that I had some knowledge and control over what I could do to make the pain and some stress go away.

Helpful Hints

Patient Tips:

Don't overschedule yourself - Give yourself a lot of time to rest, more time than you think you need. Scale back on all activities, allowing yourself to truly rest. Go so far as to reduce your work schedule - Doing so allows you to focus on how you feel with treatment.

Decrease your social circle - This allows you to know when it's okay to schedule visits for when you know you would feel good.

Designate a communicator - For me, I asked my husband and sister to take care of communicating with others, so I didn't feel overwhelmed about having to communicate the same story of what I was doing or going through over and over again.

Caregiver Tips:

Create a list of healing modalities if you haven't already - Check out the hospital's integrative health services or visit a local naturopath to learn about healing experiences ranging from yoga, reiki and acupuncture to holistic medications.

See the master list of creative gestures, gifts and ideas to help a patient in need in chapter 3.

Call to *listen*, not to learn – Calling to connect is wonderful, but don't expect the patient to update you.

Chapter 8

Finding Joy in the Little Things

Ever since I was a kid, I would make wishes on pennies. Whether it was the fountain by the local bank or a national monument with a huge bird pool, I would grab a penny, close my eyes, make a wish and throw it in. Every single time, I would say to myself, "I wish to be happy." And with a calming feeling coming over me, I would walk away with confidence and excitement for my day to come.

What I didn't realize in these childhood years was that I created a positive tool for myself. This penny-wishing act – a moment of a positive affirmation – would kick-start a good afternoon. It was a calming feeling that I gave myself, by asking the world, the universe, the pennies in the fountain to help me find happiness.

I didn't realize that first night of my diagnosis (when I couldn't fall asleep) I was chanting a positive mantra: "If Mary Ann could do it, I can too. If Mary Ann could do it, I can too." The mind is a powerful tool, and easing it can be as simple as a soothing mantra. Making a wish on a penny doesn't change the world, but a positive mindset can change a person's day. So when I was diagnosed with cancer, I did the same thing I had done as a child: I sought to find ways to create joy.

After the first few weeks of overwhelming visits and decision making, we had a plan and little extra time. And when I had extra time (and even when I didn't), I wanted to smile. I wanted to giggle. I wanted to feel overwhelming positivity to neutralize the physical pain or stressful mental anguish. And more often than not, it worked!

Once again, I was establishing a pattern that's powerful and effective. A pattern of positivity. Simplicity. I asked myself, *What makes me happy? What activities can I do on a small scale to make me smile through the hardship of living with, and treating, cancer?*

I did this because I like to smile...because I find that everything is a little better when I have a moment of joy.

I sought out those small nuggets of delight that helped me feel better momentarily. At times, it felt like everything that came with being "a girl with cancer" was so exhausting. I created virtual dance parties and requested loving personal videos from my best friends from around the county in an effort to push aside the fear and pass time before scan results. So quick pick-me-ups like buying lip gloss became extremely important.

These activities made me smile, laugh, and feel loved. Each time I allowed myself to have a little fun, I was infused with a new batch of positive energy that helped me move forward on my overwhelming to-do cancer list.

I realize that sunshine is my mojo and may not be yours. However, being around positivity is uplifting, and we all have the power of choice. As hard as it might be at times, we can choose to wake up in the morning and be in a good mood. Despite bad weather, a burnt breakfast or any other seemingly annoying moment we encounter, we can choose to not let it bring down our day. Even when we are living with and through cancer.

I'm not saying it's easy, although I am shouting from the mountaintops that *without a doubt, it's worth a try.* Choosing joy and happiness works, even if it's only for a few minutes a day.

I chose to laugh hysterically as I let my husband shave my thinning hair – I never, would have imagined a big "C" would be carved on the side of my head one day! And I nearly peed in my pants the time my three-year-old niece walked over to me with *my* wig on *her* head and told me that she looked pretty.

These times, these "little things," made me laugh and feel loved.

I just wanted to smile, even when I was having a hard time. Life isn't always easy; I know that, and so do you. But I also know that we can all choose our attitudes – I choose joy. I deliberately and consciously found ways to incorporate love and laughter in my life, and now I want *you* to give it a try.

Figure out the little things that make you happy, and find a way to include some of them in each and every day.

Here's a list of mine to jump-start your brainstorm: http:// prettywellness.com/lipstick-and-dancing/

Helpful Hints

Patient and Caregiver* Tips:

Create a bag of fun – or as my cousin Nikki calls it, a "sunshine box."

Gather bright yellow items (socks, T-shirts, underwear, pajamas) as well as inspirational books, magazines, and lists of shows, podcasts, movies that make you smile. Keep them handy (stream them on your device if they're visual) for when you are waiting in doctor's offices, on a long commute/drive, or snuggled up on your couch.

Be selective with your in-person circle

Keep your circle small – do ensure they have a positive spirit. Keep out those who bring you down. You will have rough days, and the sunshine of a positive spirit will reflect on you and help you get through.

Celebrate the little things

Every new appointment, every finished treatment, every new moon, every person holding the door open, everybody greeting to you, every new day is a reason to celebrate. Figure out what that looks like to you.

Seek help

There are many decisions to be made in a short time when dealing with cancer. Stress can be high and depression, sadness and anxiety may play a bigger role in your life than before. Seeking professional help from a mental health practitioner or supervised support groups is highly advised. Ask a doctor or insurance agent for guidance and a good recommendation near you.

Journal

Writing often can be incredibly cathartic. Throughout my life, I've journaled and found that I better understand myself when I write down my thoughts and feelings and then reflect. If nothing else, getting my fears and feelings out on paper makes me feel better. It's also provided guidance when I'm helping others in a similar position and even writing this book.

*Caregivers – Please remember to be kind and take care of yourselves, too. It's stressful for you and important that you find a little relaxation and joy along the way.

Chapter 9

Take Small Steps to Take Care of Yourself

Nine years after my initial diagnosis, I found out my cancer returned. It was the summer of my 40ᵗʰ birthday. Most of my friends organized great vacation escapes to celebrate the new decade. I, on the other hand, spent our celebration money on a full-day doctor's appointment at the Princeton Longevity Center. After a physical exam, EKG, bone scan, CAT scan and doctor's meeting, the summary was that I had the body (heart) of a 29-year old (yippee) and a suspicious lesion on my sternum. Fast-forward one month and the conclusion – stage IV, metastatic breast cancer – the same one from 2004. Being a cancer survivor, I thought I was well-versed. I was aware of the statistic – one out of eight people would be diagnosed with breast cancer – but I didn't know that nearly 30 percent of the survivors would get a reoccurrence.

Shell-shocked to hear that I had stage IV disease, I shut down for two days. The diagnosis shook Kevin and me, and yet I also knew I simply couldn't live in what-if-bad-things-happen-to-me-land. So,

I did what I do best: **I mourned without care for a few days – and then bounced back to plan my new cancer life.**

I scheduled first, second, and third opinions.

I looked at what I could control, and how could I keep my attitude in a high place.

I used my resourceful business skills and got to work figuring out my cancer life plan. I learned that lifestyle changes can influence not only how we feel daily, but also affect our longevity. So I put my head down and researched survivors thriving with disease. I studied and received a plant-based nutrition certification.

With help from my family and close friends, PrettyWellness. com, the website, was launched to create a community that included research, experience, meetings, interviews, observations, thoughts, and goofy moments on the journey toward wellness. The past few years the community has grown and Pretty Wellness is now a healthy lifestyle company that creates seminars, keynote speeches and digital content to inspire women toward resiliency, positivity and wellness.

Whether it's due to the conventional treatment, plant-based diet, daily power walk, or positive mindset, I'm thriving with stage IV disease. While I'm doing very well, I'm also aware that we need more research, so that there will be more treatments for cancer patients when current ones fail. My cancer may go away, or may not, but I'm hoping to live a long life with or without it. And I'm eternally grateful to The Cancer Couch Foundation for identifying brilliant researchers and doctors that are paving the way for better metastatic breast cancer treatments.

For me, what used to be about being pretty is now about being well. Many of the wellness tactics I now use I had heard of before, but didn't take seriously. Now I love to try, share, and inspire others to embrace health modalities and take better care of themselves so they can thrive in their own lives.

I hope and pray that you or your loved one does not get a recurrence of this disease. Many will not, luckily these people will be one and done. Either way, do NOT worry. Instead, decide on the life you want to live – and live it. Don't worry about statistics, because *you are not one.* **Learn how to take care of yourself during and after this diagnosis so that you can be happy and healthy in the life you want to live.**

The first time I was diagnosed with cancer, I took care of myself during initial diagnosis and treatment. After I concluded treatments, I jumped back into my chaotic corporate life. I ate out of vending machines, drank a ton of sugar, didn't exercise much, lived with stress on my chest, and kept rushing through life.

Well, I learned after my second diagnosis that I had an opportunity to reduce the chance of my cancer recurrence by changing my lifestyle. I wish I would have done so then (after the first time)…so I'm here to encourage *you* to do it.

I'm currently writing my next book that will shine the light on a SMALL steps approach toward better health, and my tips on surviving and thriving through hardship. I've learned that there is no one superfood or super protector from disease and hardship. I've learned to focus on wellness modalities to take care of myself. I share these daily on @PrettyWellness on Instagram providing daily tips and inspiration about taking better care of yourself. Please do so. Please reach out, follow, connect and let us know your questions about health and happiness.

I hope I have succeeded in being the soul sister who understands what you, your friends, your caregiver(s), and your family are going through, while also providing advice on how to make those initial weeks easier after a cancer diagnosis. Living through cancer isn't easy, but the truth is, *finding a little happiness through the hardship is possible.* It's a choice, and you can choose to do it.

Sending you peace, love, and healing vibes.
– *Caryn Sullivan, October 1, 2018*

30+ Small Steps Toward Better Health

CLEAN EATING

1. Put smoothies in the freezer - grab and go in the morning for an afternoon snack.
2. Freeze grapes or pineapple bites for a quick, healthy candy-like snack.
3. Love avocados? For a fresh one, pick stem off and look for bright green color.
4. Bake eggs in muffin tins for healthy morning bites.
5. Pack healthy snacks in your car, desk or purse (dried/dehydrated fruit, seeds, bagged veggies, kale chips, etc.)
6. Make a huge whole grain salad and use for three meals: stand alone, on lettuce and in broth.
7. Need to detox? Start your day with warm water and lemon.
8. Want to drink more water? Infuse it with sweet fruits and herbs or add (edible) essential oils.
9. Get your kids involved - visit farmer's markets, local farms or grocery stores together.
10. Create fun activities around clean-eating - cooking competitions / smoothie parties.

ACTIVE LIVING - MIND & BODY

11. Sleep in workout clothes so you are ready to exercise when the alarm rings.
12. Add wrist weights while blow drying your hair for a strength training sequence.
13. Do squats while you brush your teeth.
14. Make yourself workout for ten minutes.
15. Keep weights at work for quick circuit breaks.
16. Start a lunch walking group at work.
17. Schedule work meetings on the go - walk and talk while discussing or brainstorming.
18. Create a circuit routine with your kids - monkey bars, playground pushups or bleacher runs.

19. Find a meditation app and try a few minutes in the parking lot before work or any destination.
20. Create a morning or bedtime routine with your roommates, spouse or kids - share positive affirmations, keep gratitude journals.
21. Set the alarm ten minutes early - wake up to a positive thought / daily affirmation.
22. Carry a mini notebook and bullet journal - create a list about your day.

NON-TOXIC LIVING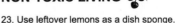

23. Use leftover lemons as a dish sponge.
24. Use baking soda to clean the oven - pour it on the bottom of oven and add a little water so it's a paste - leave on overnight for a simple wipe off.
25. Boil cinnamon in a saucepan for a fresh house scent.
26. Rub peppermint essential oil on temples for a headache.
27. Use your favorite essential oil and water in a spray bottle for a bathroom freshener mist.
28. Use essential oils on wool dryer balls for a non-toxic, sweet smelling fabric softener.
29. Make baking soda and water paste for a tough spot stain remover.
30. Use cold-pressed organic coconut oil as a hair conditioner - apply before shampooing.
31. Use cold-pressed organic coconut or sesame oil and gargle 5-20 minutes for whiter teeth - this is called oil pulling.
32. Use cold-pressed organic coconut or extra virgin olive oil for other easy beauty fixes - removing makeup, touching up flyaway hair, moisturizing the body.

Include your doctors and medical team when making lifestyle changes. It's important to always consult with a doctor before making any significant ones.

Follow us on social media @PrettyWellness
www.prettywellness.com   www.carynsullivan.com

Acknowledgements

There are so many people I would like to thank for enriching my life. I've always been a student of the world, so every teacher, camp counselor, coach, dance/music instructor, and boss played a role in my life – and I thank you for letting me in.

To my angels, Ellen, Mary Ann and Meghan, you showed me the light and how to live with and through cancer when I was first diagnosed. *This book is dedicated to you three.* You made this book possible because you guided me through those first few weeks and I lived through cancer gracefully and with joy.

To my wellness team - Thank you, Dr. Ward, Dr. Lee, Dr. Rubins, Dr. DiGiovanna, Michele Speer, Michelle Corso, Dr. C. Knowlton, Dr. Husain, Dr. Boyd, Dr. Hessberger, and Dr. M. Robbins. Thank you for letting me be me…in my serious and silly ways. I'm grateful every day that you saved my life.

To my childhood friends and your families, college buddies, and former colleagues who became dear friends, you called me from afar and sent packages, changed meetings to take me on escapades, and made sure you connected with me *no matter the distance.* You will always hold a special place in my heart especially my first survivor sisters, Rita L. E. and Nancy B. for being there within days after my original diagnosis. Lots of love to KOY, HBL, EGZ, CHD, JHL, MBR, SV, too.

To my new neighbors and this amazing community in which we live from the MOMbies to the Fairfield B.GOOD family, thank you for helping Kevin and me through the recent trials and tribulations of being a cancer patient...and for giving us a ton of hugs along the way. KWL, CM, LS, MH, MCS.

To Grandma Ceil, my biggest cheerleader, thank you for always showering me with superlatives. Everything I did was "wonderful," "terrific," "fantastic," or "spectacular." And to my Aunt Jane and Paula - thanks for sharing Grandma's zest for life with me.

To my parents, thank you for teaching me the importance of taking care of myself and not taking "no" for an answer. You have always shown an incredible amount of support even when I tried not to let you. I love you a bushel and a peck and a million hugs around the neck.

To my in-laws, thank you for loving me like your own child. You have been through the day-to-day more than anyone. I appreciate all the time and energy you have given to us time and time again. Xoxo to Libbey, and a big hug to your mom for showing me love and investigating treatments for me.

To Amy, and to eleven years of priceless next-door living with you, Nick, Nicholas, and Sophie, I truly cherish you, them, and for that chapter of my life. Your hands-on help was instrumental in our care with the cancer as well as many other milestone events.

To the family I married into – Auntie Ev, Uncle Jim, Jules, Chris, Jeff, Nikki, and Beth – Kevin and I are so blessed to have you a part of our lives. You have made Kevin laugh for years, and you've nourished our hearts, souls, and stomachs time after time. And to the Sullivans - you are the World's Greatest Family, one filled with hugs, laughs, and lots of homemade beer.

To Rebecca, I'm sorry that we've had to meet through this horrible disease. I'm in awe of your commitment to finding a cure or better treatments for stage IV. *To health and sanity, my friend!*

The Cancer Couch Foundation will help us and many more live and thrive.

To Jackie, thank you for pushing Reb and me to be friends, and for always being both of our biggest cheerleaders in work and in life. *Because of that, our lives will live longer.* Because of all you to support us in treatment, our sanity is a little calmer. You have the biggest heart. I-V-III to you and Caroline – and Caroline, you are another dear friend for whom I'm grateful.

To my business-mentors-turned-close-friends, all the way from Sesame Street Live and Disney/ESPN especially Stacey, Jane, Michelle, Lori, Robyn, and Susan - Thank you for all the love and guidance you continually have shown me throughout the decades. Thank you for dropping everything, whether it's during a bad cancer diagnosis or a revision of my book, speaking presentation, entrepreneurial project...or even to babysit my kid. (xoxo SM)

To my BFF Michele, I'm honored that we have been such genuine, heartfelt, best friends for so long. Through the years you've helped me grow my career strategically, and now you do the same for my entrepreneurial ventures. You've supported me through a myriad of young adult antics, and the joys of parenting. You challenge me in every area of my life, and I'm beyond grateful that you are a continual part of it.

To my brother-in-law Matt, you have saved my life on numerous occasions. I can't express how grateful I am for the time you have spent on my case. I'm incredibly blessed that you are in our lives. Thank you.

To my little sister, Nancy, I never saw cancer being a part of our story. After Grandpa Lou died, I thought I would fall apart if I ever had cancer too – but you kept me together many times throughout. Your research was instrumental in the decision-making. Your thoughtful presence after the original surgery – and then the presents all the time – kept me smiling. You are a brilliant and truly beautiful person inside and out. Thanks for always having faith in me.

To Kyle, you are our miracle, and I'm so very proud of the person you have become. Your kind spirit and big smile makes every single person who connects with you feel comfortable. I love you more than you love...

Last but certainly not least, Kevin. You are my rock. You are my calm through any storms – cancer or not. You are wise beyond what I could have imagined, and have handled so many of our life situations with grace. You have taught me how to love unconditionally and how to be a great parent. My life has such depth and meaning because of you. I love you more than 10,000...

Journal

Today _____
(date)

How I feel ☺ ☺ ☺ ☹ ☹

My thoughts

_____
_____
_____
_____
_____
_____
_____
_____
_____
_____
_____
_____
_____
_____
_____
_____
_____

This made me smile _____
_____

One nice thing I will do for myself tomorrow _____
_____

Today

_____

(date)

How I feel   ☺ ☺ ☺ ☹ ☹

My thoughts

_____

_____

_____

_____

_____

_____

_____

_____

_____

_____

_____

_____

_____

_____

_____

_____

_____

This made me smile _____

_____

One nice thing I will do for myself tomorrow _____

_____

Today

_____
(date)

How I feel   ☺ ☺ ☺ ☹ ☹

My thoughts

_____
_____
_____
_____
_____
_____
_____
_____
_____
_____
_____
_____
_____
_____
_____
_____
_____

This made me smile _____
_____

One nice thing I will do for myself tomorrow _____
_____

Today _____
(date)

How I feel   ☺   ☺   😐   ☹   ☹

My thoughts

_____

_____

_____

_____

_____

_____

_____

_____

_____

_____

_____

_____

_____

_____

_____

_____

This made me smile _____

_____

One nice thing I will do for myself tomorrow _____

_____

Today _____
(date)

How I feel ☺ ☺ ☺ ☹ ☹

My thoughts

_____
_____
_____
_____
_____
_____
_____
_____
_____
_____
_____
_____
_____
_____
_____
_____

This made me smile _____

One nice thing I will do for myself tomorrow _____
_____

Today _____
(date)

How I feel　　　😊　😊　😐　☹️　☹️

My thoughts

_____
_____
_____
_____
_____
_____
_____
_____
_____
_____
_____
_____
_____
_____
_____
_____
_____

This made me smile _____
_____

One nice thing I will do for myself tomorrow _____
_____

Today ⎯⎯⎯⎯⎯⎯⎯⎯⎯⎯⎯⎯
(date)

How I feel ☺ ☺ ☐ ☹ ☹

My thoughts

⎯⎯⎯⎯⎯⎯⎯⎯⎯⎯⎯⎯⎯⎯⎯⎯⎯⎯⎯⎯⎯⎯⎯⎯⎯⎯⎯
⎯⎯⎯⎯⎯⎯⎯⎯⎯⎯⎯⎯⎯⎯⎯⎯⎯⎯⎯⎯⎯⎯⎯⎯⎯⎯⎯
⎯⎯⎯⎯⎯⎯⎯⎯⎯⎯⎯⎯⎯⎯⎯⎯⎯⎯⎯⎯⎯⎯⎯⎯⎯⎯⎯
⎯⎯⎯⎯⎯⎯⎯⎯⎯⎯⎯⎯⎯⎯⎯⎯⎯⎯⎯⎯⎯⎯⎯⎯⎯⎯⎯
⎯⎯⎯⎯⎯⎯⎯⎯⎯⎯⎯⎯⎯⎯⎯⎯⎯⎯⎯⎯⎯⎯⎯⎯⎯⎯⎯
⎯⎯⎯⎯⎯⎯⎯⎯⎯⎯⎯⎯⎯⎯⎯⎯⎯⎯⎯⎯⎯⎯⎯⎯⎯⎯⎯
⎯⎯⎯⎯⎯⎯⎯⎯⎯⎯⎯⎯⎯⎯⎯⎯⎯⎯⎯⎯⎯⎯⎯⎯⎯⎯⎯
⎯⎯⎯⎯⎯⎯⎯⎯⎯⎯⎯⎯⎯⎯⎯⎯⎯⎯⎯⎯⎯⎯⎯⎯⎯⎯⎯
⎯⎯⎯⎯⎯⎯⎯⎯⎯⎯⎯⎯⎯⎯⎯⎯⎯⎯⎯⎯⎯⎯⎯⎯⎯⎯⎯
⎯⎯⎯⎯⎯⎯⎯⎯⎯⎯⎯⎯⎯⎯⎯⎯⎯⎯⎯⎯⎯⎯⎯⎯⎯⎯⎯
⎯⎯⎯⎯⎯⎯⎯⎯⎯⎯⎯⎯⎯⎯⎯⎯⎯⎯⎯⎯⎯⎯⎯⎯⎯⎯⎯
⎯⎯⎯⎯⎯⎯⎯⎯⎯⎯⎯⎯⎯⎯⎯⎯⎯⎯⎯⎯⎯⎯⎯⎯⎯⎯⎯

This made me smile ⎯⎯⎯⎯⎯⎯⎯⎯⎯⎯⎯⎯⎯⎯⎯
⎯⎯⎯⎯⎯⎯⎯⎯⎯⎯⎯⎯⎯⎯⎯⎯⎯⎯⎯⎯⎯⎯⎯⎯⎯⎯⎯

One nice thing I will do for myself tomorrow ⎯⎯⎯⎯⎯
⎯⎯⎯⎯⎯⎯⎯⎯⎯⎯⎯⎯⎯⎯⎯⎯⎯⎯⎯⎯⎯⎯⎯⎯⎯⎯⎯

Today _____
(date)

How I feel ☺ ☺ 😐 ☹ ☹

My thoughts

_____
_____
_____
_____
_____
_____
_____
_____
_____
_____
_____
_____
_____
_____
_____
_____
_____

This made me smile _____
_____

One nice thing I will do for myself tomorrow _____
_____

Today _____
(date)

How I feel   ☺ ☺ 😐 ☹ ☹

My thoughts

_____
_____
_____
_____
_____
_____
_____
_____
_____
_____
_____
_____
_____
_____
_____
_____

This made me smile _____
_____

One nice thing I will do for myself tomorrow _____
_____

Today _____
(date)

How I feel   ☺ ☺ ☺ ☹ ☹

My thoughts

_____
_____
_____
_____
_____
_____
_____
_____
_____
_____
_____
_____
_____
_____
_____
_____
_____
_____

This made me smile _____
_____

One nice thing I will do for myself tomorrow _____
_____

Today _____
(date)

How I feel 😊 🙂 😐 🙁 ☹️

My thoughts

_____
_____
_____
_____
_____
_____
_____
_____
_____
_____
_____
_____
_____
_____
_____
_____
_____
_____

This made me smile _____
_____

One nice thing I will do for myself tomorrow _____
_____

Today _____
(date)

How I feel   ☺ ☺ ☺ ☹ ☹

My thoughts

_____
_____
_____
_____
_____
_____
_____
_____
_____
_____
_____
_____
_____
_____
_____
_____

This made me smile _____
_____

One nice thing I will do for myself tomorrow _____
_____

Today _____
(date)

How I feel   ☺ ☺ 😐 ☹ ☹

My thoughts

_____
_____
_____
_____
_____
_____
_____
_____
_____
_____
_____
_____
_____
_____
_____
_____

This made me smile _____
_____

One nice thing I will do for myself tomorrow _____
_____

Today _____
(date)

How I feel   ☺ ☺ 😐 ☹ ☹

My thoughts

_____

_____

_____

_____

_____

_____

_____

_____

_____

_____

_____

_____

_____

_____

_____

_____

This made me smile _____

_____

One nice thing I will do for myself tomorrow _____

_____

Today _____
(date)

How I feel   ☺   ☺   😐   ☹   ☹

My thoughts

_____

_____

_____

_____

_____

_____

_____

_____

_____

_____

_____

_____

_____

_____

_____

_____

This made me smile _____

_____

One nice thing I will do for myself tomorrow _____

_____

Today _____
(date)

How I feel   ☺ ☺ 😐 ☹ ☹

My thoughts

_____
_____
_____
_____
_____
_____
_____
_____
_____
_____
_____
_____
_____
_____
_____

This made me smile _____
_____

One nice thing I will do for myself tomorrow _____
_____

Today _____
(date)

How I feel   ☺ ☺ 😐 ☹ ☹

My thoughts

_____
_____
_____
_____
_____
_____
_____
_____
_____
_____
_____
_____
_____
_____
_____

This made me smile _____
_____

One nice thing I will do for myself tomorrow _____
_____

Today _____
(date)

How I feel   🙂   🙂   😐   🙁   🙁

My thoughts

_____

_____

_____

_____

_____

_____

_____

_____

_____

_____

_____

_____

_____

_____

_____

_____

_____

This made me smile _____

_____

One nice thing I will do for myself tomorrow _____

_____

Today

_____
(date)

How I feel ☺ ☺ 😐 ☹ ☹

My thoughts

_____
_____
_____
_____
_____
_____
_____
_____
_____
_____
_____
_____
_____
_____
_____
_____
_____
_____

This made me smile _____

_____

One nice thing I will do for myself tomorrow _____

_____

Today

_____
(date)

How I feel   ☺ ☺ 😐 ☹ ☹

My thoughts

_____
_____
_____
_____
_____
_____
_____
_____
_____
_____
_____
_____
_____
_____
_____
_____
_____

This made me smile _____
_____

One nice thing I will do for myself tomorrow _____
_____

Today _____
(date)

How I feel   

My thoughts

_____
_____
_____
_____
_____
_____
_____
_____
_____
_____
_____
_____
_____
_____
_____
_____
_____
_____

This made me smile _____

_____

One nice thing I will do for myself tomorrow _____

_____

Today _____
(date)

How I feel   ☺ ☺ 😐 ☹ ☹

My thoughts

_____
_____
_____
_____
_____
_____
_____
_____
_____
_____
_____
_____
_____
_____
_____
_____

This made me smile _____
_____

One nice thing I will do for myself tomorrow _____
_____

Today _____

How I feel

My thoughts

_____
_____
_____
_____
_____
_____
_____
_____
_____
_____
_____
_____
_____
_____
_____
_____

This made me smile _____
_____

One nice thing I will do for myself tomorrow _____
_____

Today _____
(date)

How I feel   😊 🙂 😐 🙁 ☹️

My thoughts

_____
_____
_____
_____
_____
_____
_____
_____
_____
_____
_____
_____
_____
_____
_____
_____

This made me smile _____

_____

One nice thing I will do for myself tomorrow _____

_____

Today _____
(date)

How I feel ☺ ☺ ☺ ☹ ☹

My thoughts

_____

_____

_____

_____

_____

_____

_____

_____

_____

_____

_____

_____

_____

_____

_____

_____

_____

This made me smile _____

_____

One nice thing I will do for myself tomorrow _____

_____

Today _____
(date)

How I feel   ☺ ☺ 😐 🙁 ☹

My thoughts

_____

_____

_____

_____

_____

_____

_____

_____

_____

_____

_____

_____

_____

_____

_____

_____

This made me smile _____

_____

One nice thing I will do for myself tomorrow _____

_____

Today _____
(date)

How I feel

My thoughts

_____

_____

_____

_____

_____

_____

_____

_____

_____

_____

_____

_____

_____

_____

_____

_____

This made me smile _____

_____

One nice thing I will do for myself tomorrow _____

_____

Today _____
(date)

How I feel   ☺ ☺ 😐 ☹ ☹

My thoughts

_____

_____

_____

_____

_____

_____

_____

_____

_____

_____

_____

_____

_____

_____

_____

This made me smile _____

_____

One nice thing I will do for myself tomorrow _____

_____

Today _____
(date)

How I feel   ☺ ☺ 😐 ☹ ☹

My thoughts

_____

_____

_____

_____

_____

_____

_____

_____

_____

_____

_____

_____

_____

_____

_____

_____

This made me smile _____

_____

One nice thing I will do for myself tomorrow _____

_____

Today _____
(date)

How I feel   ☺   ☺   😐   ☹   ☹

My thoughts

_____

_____

_____

_____

_____

_____

_____

_____

_____

_____

_____

_____

_____

_____

_____

_____

_____

This made me smile _____

_____

One nice thing I will do for myself tomorrow _____

_____

Today _____
(date)

How I feel   ☺ ☺ 😐 ☹ ☹

My thoughts

_____
_____
_____
_____
_____
_____
_____
_____
_____
_____
_____
_____
_____
_____

This made me smile _____
_____

One nice thing I will do for myself tomorrow _____
_____

Today _____
(date)

How I feel ☺ ☺ ☺ ☹ ☹

My thoughts

_____
_____
_____
_____
_____
_____
_____
_____
_____
_____
_____
_____
_____
_____
_____
_____
_____
_____

This made me smile _____

_____

One nice thing I will do for myself tomorrow _____

_____

Today

_____
(date)

How I feel   ☺ ☺ 😐 ☹ ☹

My thoughts

_____
_____
_____
_____
_____
_____
_____
_____
_____
_____
_____
_____
_____
_____
_____
_____

This made me smile _____
_____

One nice thing I will do for myself tomorrow _____
_____

Today _____
(date)

How I feel   ☺ ☺ ☺ ☹ ☹

My thoughts

_____
_____
_____
_____
_____
_____
_____
_____
_____
_____
_____
_____
_____
_____
_____

This made me smile _____
_____

One nice thing I will do for myself tomorrow _____
_____

Today _____
(date)

How I feel ☺ ☺ 😐 🙁 ☹

My thoughts

_____
_____
_____
_____
_____
_____
_____
_____
_____
_____
_____
_____
_____
_____
_____
_____

This made me smile _____
_____

One nice thing I will do for myself tomorrow _____
_____

Today

_____
(date)

How I feel ☺ ☺ ☺ ☹ ☹

My thoughts

_____

_____

_____

_____

_____

_____

_____

_____

_____

_____

_____

_____

_____

_____

_____

_____

This made me smile _____

_____

One nice thing I will do for myself tomorrow _____

_____

Today _____
(date)

How I feel   ☺ ☺ 😐 ☹ ☹

My thoughts

_____
_____
_____
_____
_____
_____
_____
_____
_____
_____
_____
_____
_____
_____
_____

This made me smile _____
_____

One nice thing I will do for myself tomorrow _____
_____

Today _____
(date)

How I feel ☺ ☺ 😐 ☹ ☹

My thoughts

_____
_____
_____
_____
_____
_____
_____
_____
_____
_____
_____
_____
_____
_____
_____
_____
_____

This made me smile _____
_____

One nice thing I will do for myself tomorrow _____
_____

Today _____
(date)

How I feel   ☺ ☺ 😐 ☹ ☹

My thoughts

_____
_____
_____
_____
_____
_____
_____
_____
_____
_____
_____
_____
_____
_____
_____
_____
_____

This made me smile _____

One nice thing I will do for myself tomorrow _____
_____

Notes

Notes

(appointment/meetings/random thoughts)

_____

_____

_____

_____

_____

_____

_____

_____

_____

_____

_____

_____

Notes

(appointment/meetings/random thoughts)

Notes

(appointment/meetings/random thoughts)

Notes

(appointment/meetings/random thoughts)

Notes

(appointment/meetings/random thoughts)

Notes

(appointment/meetings/random thoughts)

Notes

(appointment/meetings/random thoughts)

Notes

(appointment/meetings/random thoughts)

Notes

(appointment/meetings/random thoughts)

_____

_____

_____

_____

_____

_____

_____

_____

_____

_____

_____

_____

Notes

(appointment/meetings/random thoughts)

_____

_____

_____

_____

_____

_____

_____

_____

_____

_____

_____

_____

_____

Notes

(appointment/meetings/random thoughts)

Notes

(appointment/meetings/random thoughts)

Notes

(appointment/meetings/random thoughts)

Notes

(appointment/meetings/random thoughts)

_____

_____

_____

_____

_____

_____

_____

_____

_____

_____

_____

_____

Notes

(appointment/meetings/random thoughts)

_____

_____

_____

_____

_____

_____

_____

_____

_____

_____

_____

_____

_____

Notes

(appointment/meetings/random thoughts)

_____

_____

_____

_____

_____

_____

_____

_____

_____

_____

_____

Notes

(appointment/meetings/random thoughts)

Notes

(appointment/meetings/random thoughts)

_____

_____

_____

_____

_____

_____

_____

_____

_____

_____

_____

_____

_____

Notes

(appointment/meetings/random thoughts)

_____

_____

_____

_____

_____

_____

_____

_____

_____

_____

_____

_____

Notes

(appointment/meetings/random thoughts)

Notes

(appointment/meetings/random thoughts)

_____

_____

_____

_____

_____

_____

_____

_____

_____

_____

_____

Notes

(appointment/meetings/random thoughts)

_____

_____

_____

_____

_____

_____

_____

_____

_____

_____

_____

Notes

(appointment/meetings/random thoughts)

Notes

(appointment/meetings/random thoughts)

_____

_____

_____

_____

_____

_____

_____

_____

_____

_____

_____

_____

Notes

(appointment/meetings/random thoughts)

Notes

(appointment/meetings/random thoughts)

_____

_____

_____

_____

_____

_____

_____

_____

_____

_____

_____

_____

Notes

(appointment/meetings/random thoughts)

_____

_____

_____

_____

_____

_____

_____

_____

_____

_____

_____

_____

_____

Notes

(appointment/meetings/random thoughts)

Notes

_____

(appointment/meetings/random thoughts)

_____

_____

_____

_____

_____

_____

_____

_____

_____

_____

_____

_____

Notes

(appointment/meetings/random thoughts)

Notes

(appointment/meetings/random thoughts)

Notes

(appointment/meetings/random thoughts)

Notes

(appointment/meetings/random thoughts)

Notes

(appointment/meetings/random thoughts)

_____

_____

_____

_____

_____

_____

_____

_____

_____

_____

_____

_____

Notes

(appointment/meetings/random thoughts)

_____

_____

_____

_____

_____

_____

_____

_____

_____

_____

_____

_____

Notes

(appointment/meetings/random thoughts)

Notes

(appointment/meetings/random thoughts)

_____

_____

_____

_____

_____

_____

_____

_____

_____

_____

_____

_____

Notes

(appointment/meetings/random thoughts)

Notes

(appointment/meetings/random thoughts)

Notes

(appointment/meetings/random thoughts)

Notes

(appointment/meetings/random thoughts)

Notes

(appointment/meetings/random thoughts)

Notes

(appointment/meetings/random thoughts)

_____

_____

_____

_____

_____

_____

_____

_____

_____

_____

_____

_____

_____

Notes

(appointment/meetings/random thoughts)

_____

_____

_____

_____

_____

_____

_____

_____

_____

_____

_____

_____

_____

Notes

(appointment/meetings/random thoughts)

Notes

(appointment/meetings/random thoughts)

_____

_____

_____

_____

_____

_____

_____

_____

_____

_____

_____

_____

Notes

(appointment/meetings/random thoughts)

_____

_____

_____

_____

_____

_____

_____

_____

_____

_____

_____

_____

_____

Notes

(appointment/meetings/random thoughts)

_____

_____

_____

_____

_____

_____

_____

_____

_____

_____

_____

_____

Notes

(appointment/meetings/random thoughts)

_____

_____

_____

_____

_____

_____

_____

_____

_____

_____

_____

_____

Notes

(appointment/meetings/random thoughts)

Notes

(appointment/meetings/random thoughts)

_____

_____

_____

_____

_____

_____

_____

_____

_____

_____

_____

_____

Notes

(appointment/meetings/random thoughts)

_____

_____

_____

_____

_____

_____

_____

_____

_____

_____

_____

_____

Notes

(appointment/meetings/random thoughts)

_____

_____

_____

_____

_____

_____

_____

_____

_____

_____

_____

_____

Notes

(appointment/meetings/random thoughts)

Notes

(appointment/meetings/random thoughts)

_____

_____

_____

_____

_____

_____

_____

_____

_____

_____

_____

_____

Notes

(appointment/meetings/random thoughts)

Notes

(appointment/meetings/random thoughts)

_____

_____

_____

_____

_____

_____

_____

_____

_____

_____

_____

_____

Notes

(appointment/meetings/random thoughts)

Notes

(appointment/meetings/random thoughts)

Notes

(appointment/meetings/random thoughts)

Notes

(appointment/meetings/random thoughts)

Notes

(appointment/meetings/random thoughts)

Notes

(appointment/meetings/random thoughts)

Notes

(appointment/meetings/random thoughts)

Notes

(appointment/meetings/random thoughts)

_____

_____

_____

_____

_____

_____

_____

_____

_____

_____

_____

_____

Notes

(appointment/meetings/random thoughts)

_____

_____

_____

_____

_____

_____

_____

_____

_____

_____

_____

_____

Notes

(appointment/meetings/random thoughts)

_____

_____

_____

_____

_____

_____

_____

_____

_____

_____

_____

_____

Notes

(appointment/meetings/random thoughts)

_____

_____

_____

_____

_____

_____

_____

_____

_____

_____

_____

_____

_____

Notes

(appointment/meetings/random thoughts)

_____

_____

_____

_____

_____

_____

_____

_____

_____

_____

_____

_____

Notes

(appointment/meetings/random thoughts)

_____

_____

_____

_____

_____

_____

_____

_____

_____

_____

_____

_____

Notes

(appointment/meetings/random thoughts)

Notes

(appointment/meetings/random thoughts)